Designed by Roni Akmon

Cover illustration by Jessie Wilcox Smith, Title Page by Maud Humphrey
Other illustrations used this book are from: Fine Art Photgraphic Library,
Balliol Corp. and the Bridgeman Art Library
Tea Time, 1904 by Arthur Elsley (1861-1952)
Fine Art of Oakham LTD. Leicestshire/Bridgeman Art Library, London

This book is dedicated to Wendy.
She spent countless hours in the kitchen
with me testing these recipes.

ISBN 1-884807-33-X

Published by Blushing Rose Publishing
P.O. 2238
San Anselmo, CA 94979

Printed and Bound in China

Come to my Tea Party
a cookbook for children

For: _____

With love from: _____

Date: _____

Written by Nancy Cogan Akmon
Designed by Roni Akmon

Blushing Rose Publishing
San Anselmo, California

Kitchen Rules .... pg. 5

How to Measure .... pg. 6

Things You Will Need .... pg. 7

Cooking Tips .... pg. 9

Tea Party Menus .... pg. 10

Setting the Table .... pg. 12

Party Decorations .... pg. 14

Breakfast & Breads .... pg. 19

Soups & Sandwiches .... pg. 31

Salads & Party Drinks .... pg. 39

Main Dishes .... pg. 45

Potatoes, Rice & Side Dishes .... pg. 59

Cookies, Cakes & Sweets .... pg. 65

My Own Recipes .... pg. 80

Recipe Index .... pg. 82

KITCHEN RULES

1) Wash your hands!

2) Have an adult standing by to help you when cutting, using the stove or taking pans out of the oven.

3) Read over the whole recipe and make sure you have all ingredients before you begin.

4) Put on an apron.

5) Measure all ingredients carefully.

6) Always use good thick pot holders when removing pans from the oven or microwave.

7) Always turn pot handles towards the center of the stove.

8) When opening the oven, turn your face away to avoid the steam. It's hot!

9) Turn off the stove or oven when finished.

10) Clean up!

11) An adult should always be in the house to assist you while cooking

HOW TO MEASURE

1 cup   ½ cup   ⅓ cup   ¼ cup

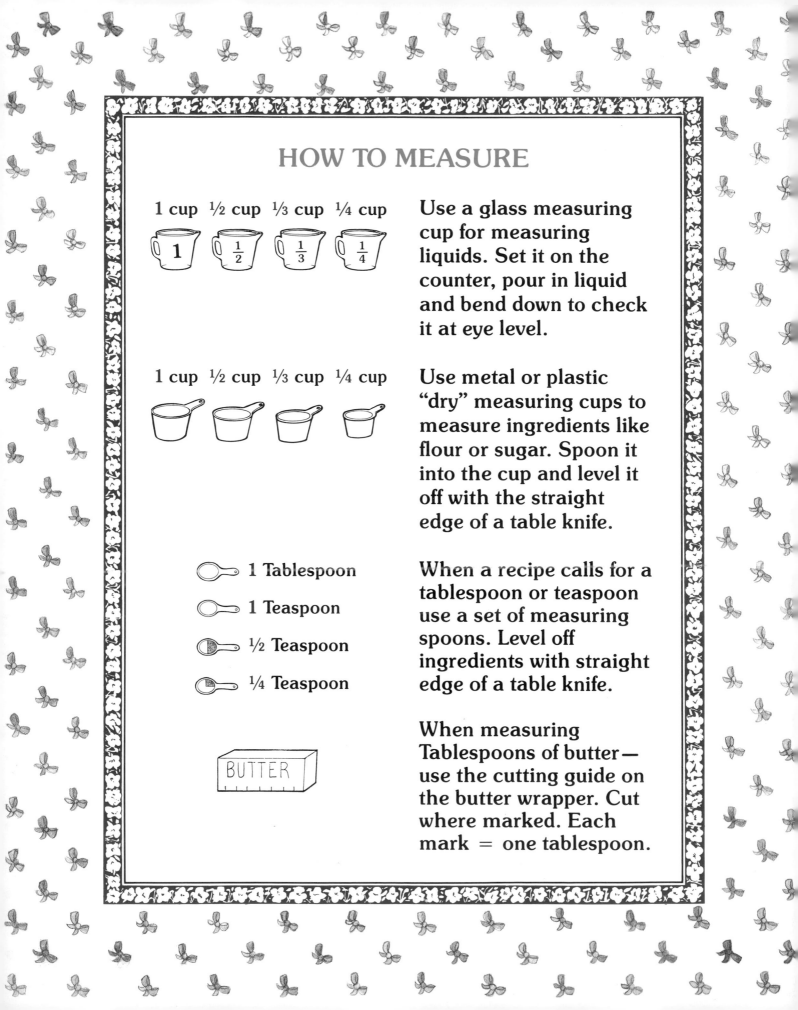

Use a glass measuring cup for measuring liquids. Set it on the counter, pour in liquid and bend down to check it at eye level.

1 cup   ½ cup   ⅓ cup   ¼ cup

Use metal or plastic "dry" measuring cups to measure ingredients like flour or sugar. Spoon it into the cup and level it off with the straight edge of a table knife.

1 Tablespoon

1 Teaspoon

½ Teaspoon

¼ Teaspoon

When a recipe calls for a tablespoon or teaspoon use a set of measuring spoons. Level off ingredients with straight edge of a table knife.

BUTTER

When measuring Tablespoons of butter — use the cutting guide on the butter wrapper. Cut where marked. Each mark = one tablespoon.

THINGS YOU WILL NEED

Small mixing bowl

Medium mixing bowl

Large mixing bowl

Sharp knife

Wooden mixing spoon

Metal spatula

Plastic spatula for non-stick pans

Rubber spatula

Wooden cutting board

Vegetable peeler

Pastry brush

Can opener

Wooden rolling pin

Electric hand mixer

Grater

Potato masher

THINGS YOU WILL NEED

Large fry pan
Medium fry
pan

Large soup pot
or "Dutch Oven"

Large,
Medium,
Small pots
with lids

Square
pan

Round
cake pan

Loaf pan

Pie plate
metal or glass

Oblong pan
13"x9"

Muffin
tin

Cookie sheet

Pot holders

Small
Microwaveable
bowl, glass or
plastic

Covered
casserole dish

COOKING TIPS

- Always bake on the center rack of the oven.

- Always use the timer when cooking or baking. Have an adult show you how to use it.

- To test cakes, muffins and quick breads, use a toothpick inserted into the center. If it comes out clean, it's done. If not, cook a few minutes more.

- The herbs rosemary, thyme, marjoram and basil can be substituted for one another in any of these recipes.

- Since microwaves vary in power, you may have to adjust microwave cooking time slightly.

- Use a plastic spatula to turn over foods, when cooking in a non-stick pan. Metal will scratch the surface.

- Whenever a recipe calls for butter, you may substitute margarine.

- When a recipe calls for melted butter, put butter into a microwaveable cup and microwave until melted.

- Use butter or oil on a paper towel to "grease" the bottoms and side of a pan.

- When a recipe says, "beat", use an electric mixer. If it says, "stir", use your wooden cooking spoon.

9

COME TO MY TEA PARTY MENUS

Breakfast Menus

Potato Omelette...pg. 21

Blueberry Muffins...pg. 25

Fruity Frost...pg. 44

Sunshine Eggs...pg. 20

Fruit Salad...pg. 41

Hot Cocoa

Lunch Menus

Chicken Noodle Soup...pg. 34

Pinwheel Sandwiches...pg. 37

Wendy's Chocolate Chip
   Cookies...pg. 66

Tacos...pg. 53

Nice Rice...pg. 60

Apple Crisp...pg. 71

Dinner Menus

Best Burgers...pg. 51

Mashed Potatoes...pg. 61

Easy Carrots...pg. 63

Tropical Banana Treat
   ...pg. 72

Creamy Clam Chowder
   ...pg. 32

Wendy's Garlic Bread
   ...pg. 29

Green Salad with Thousand
   Island Dressing...pg. 42

Orange Sherbet Cups
   ...pg. 73

COME TO MY TEA PARTY MENUS

Picnic Menus

Shake & Bake Sesame
Chicken...pg. 47

Potato Salad...pg. 40

Lemon Glaze Cake...pg. 67

Barbequed Chicken Wings
...pg. 49

Easy Corn Bread...pg. 28

Fresh Fruit/Divine Peanut
Butter Balls...pg. 79

Tea Party Menus

Tea Party Sandwiches
...pg. 15

Fantasy Fruits...pg. 77

Stained Glass Sugar
Cookies...pg. 78

Topsy Turnovers...pg. 56

Cherry Cheesecake Pie
...pg. 17

7 Layer Cookies...pg. 81

Lunchbox Menus

Mom's Tuna Boats...pg. 35

Fresh Fruit

Marchmallow Crispie
Treats ...pg. 69

Quesadillas...pg. 54

Ants on a Log...pg. 68

Chocolate Peanut Butter
Chip Cookies...pg. 75

SETTING THE TABLE

To set the table, place your napkin and fork to the left of the plate. Your knife and spoon go on the right. The sharp edge of the knife faces the plate. The glass is set above the knife.

LET'S HAVE A TEA PARTY

Invite your friends and family to a wonderful tea party. Serve tea, scones with jam, tea party sandwiches, and a special cake like our cherry cheesecake or choose one of the cookie recipes in the dessert section.

Decorate the table with fresh flowers and set each place with a pretty china plate, teacup and saucer, napkin, fork, knife and teaspoon. Serve the tea party sandwiches on a platter decorated with a doily. Place the scones in a basket lined with a linen napkin. Put some jam in a small serving bowl. Put the dessert on a decorative plate and place onto the table along with the sandwiches, scones and jam.

You may serve tea, cocoa, or lemonade in your teacups at your tea party. Herbal teas, which do not have caffeine, are also a good choice. To make delicious tea: boil water in a kettle. Place 2 teabags into a teapot, and with an adult's help, pour the hot water into the teapot. Let steep for 4 minutes. You're now ready to serve the tea. Pour some milk into a small pitcher. Cut a lemon into thin slices and place them onto a small plate. Now place the teapot, milk, and lemon onto the table along with a sugar bowl, and you're ready for the tea party!

13

PARTY DECORATIONS

Pick 3 or 4 party theme colors and use these colors throughout. Fill your party room with beautiful colored balloons tied with long dangling ribbons and hang crepe paper streamers. (You will need thumb tacks to secure streamers).

Coordinate with matching decorative tablecloth, paper plates, napkins and cups. Sprinkle confetti on the table and add a vase of flowers for a festive touch. Music and lighting are also important. Christmas tree lights can add a beautiful special effect to your party.

Pick a special menu for your party (including drinks) and serve the food attractively on trays, lined with doilies, or decorated with flowers. Serve breads in baskets lined with the matching party napkins. Use your imagination to make the party your own very special event!

TEA PARTY SANDWICHES

Cream Cheese and Cucumber:

¼ cup cream cheese

cucumber slices

8   slices white bread

Egg Salad:

3   eggs

¼ cup mayonnaise

¼ teaspoon curry powder

salt and pepper

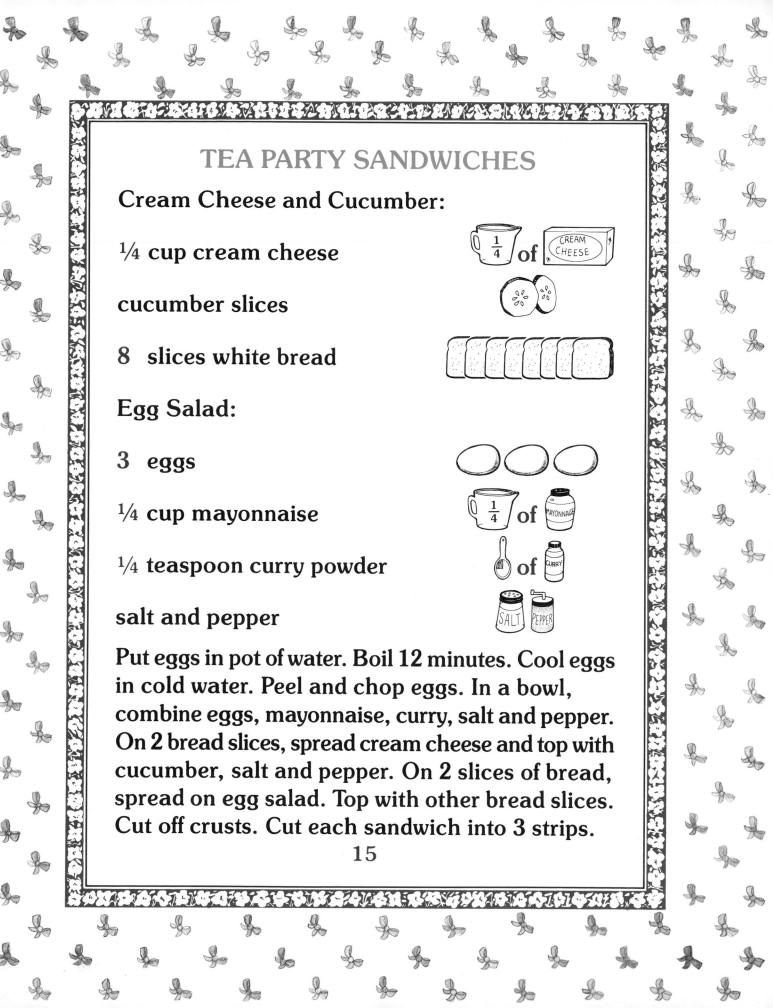

Put eggs in pot of water. Boil 12 minutes. Cool eggs in cold water. Peel and chop eggs. In a bowl, combine eggs, mayonnaise, curry, salt and pepper. On 2 bread slices, spread cream cheese and top with cucumber, salt and pepper. On 2 slices of bread, spread on egg salad. Top with other bread slices. Cut off crusts. Cut each sandwich into 3 strips.

15

GOLDEN RAISIN SCONES

2½ cups flour

¼ cup sugar

1 tablespoon baking powder

1 stick butter

2 large eggs

⅓ cup milk

⅔ cup golden raisins

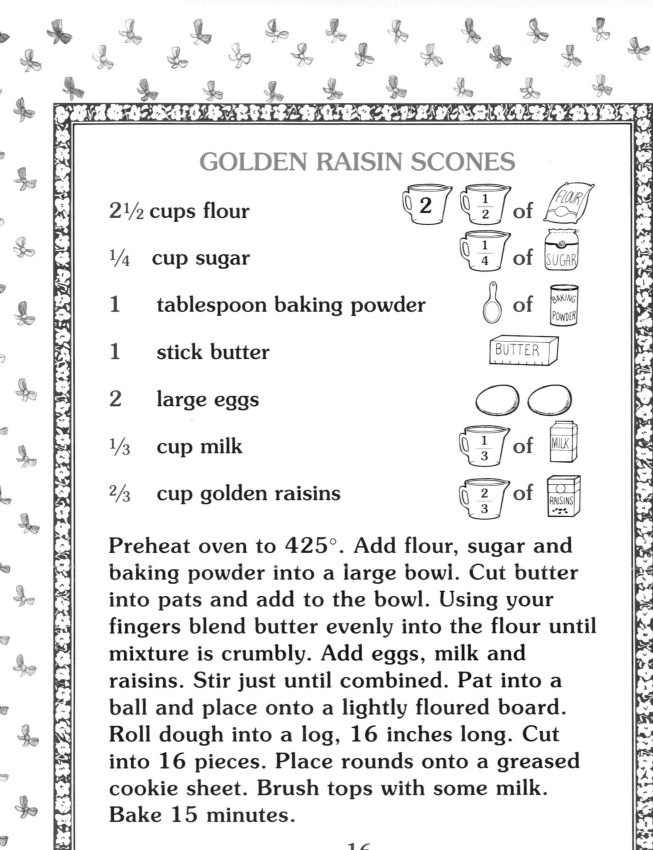

Preheat oven to 425°. Add flour, sugar and baking powder into a large bowl. Cut butter into pats and add to the bowl. Using your fingers blend butter evenly into the flour until mixture is crumbly. Add eggs, milk and raisins. Stir just until combined. Pat into a ball and place onto a lightly floured board. Roll dough into a log, 16 inches long. Cut into 16 pieces. Place rounds onto a greased cookie sheet. Brush tops with some milk. Bake 15 minutes.

CHERRY CHEESECAKE PIE

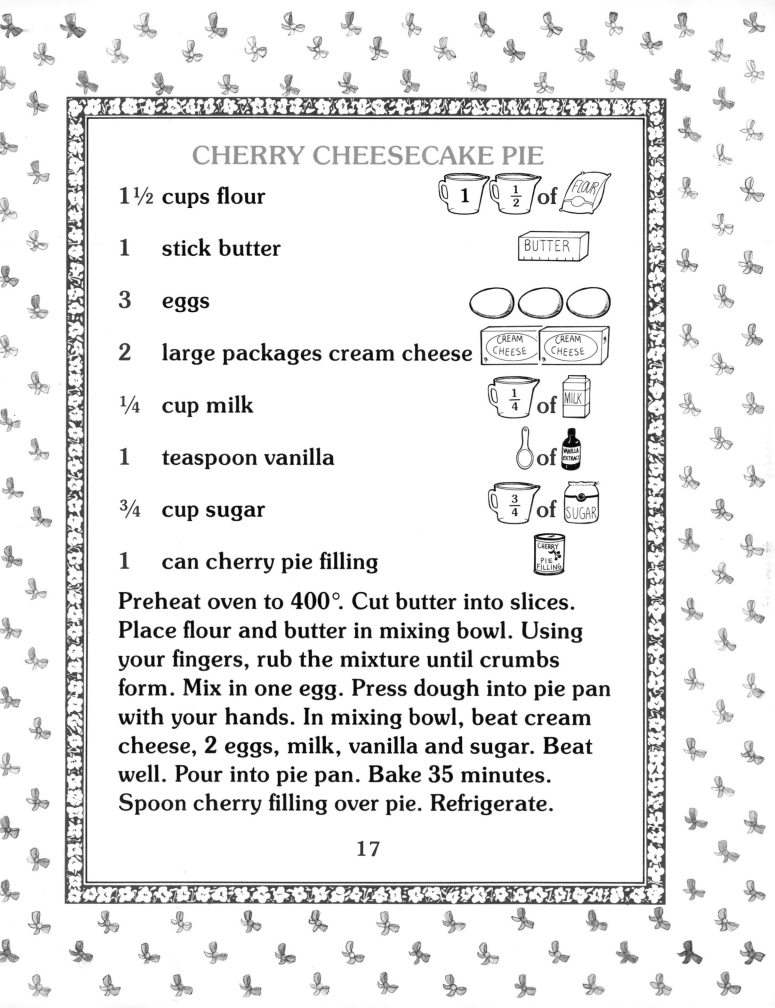

1½ cups flour

1 stick butter

3 eggs

2 large packages cream cheese

¼ cup milk

1 teaspoon vanilla

¾ cup sugar

1 can cherry pie filling

Preheat oven to 400°. Cut butter into slices. Place flour and butter in mixing bowl. Using your fingers, rub the mixture until crumbs form. Mix in one egg. Press dough into pie pan with your hands. In mixing bowl, beat cream cheese, 2 eggs, milk, vanilla and sugar. Beat well. Pour into pie pan. Bake 35 minutes. Spoon cherry filling over pie. Refrigerate.

17

CHAPTER 1

Breakfast & Breads

19

SUNSHINE EGGS

2   pieces of bread

2   eggs

1   tablespoon butter

salt & pepper

Cut a hole in each piece of bread with a cookie cutter. Put butter in a large fry pan on medium heat. Put bread in the pan. Break eggs into the holes of the bread. Cook for 2 minutes. Turn over. Sprinkle with salt and pepper and serve.

POTATO OMELETTE

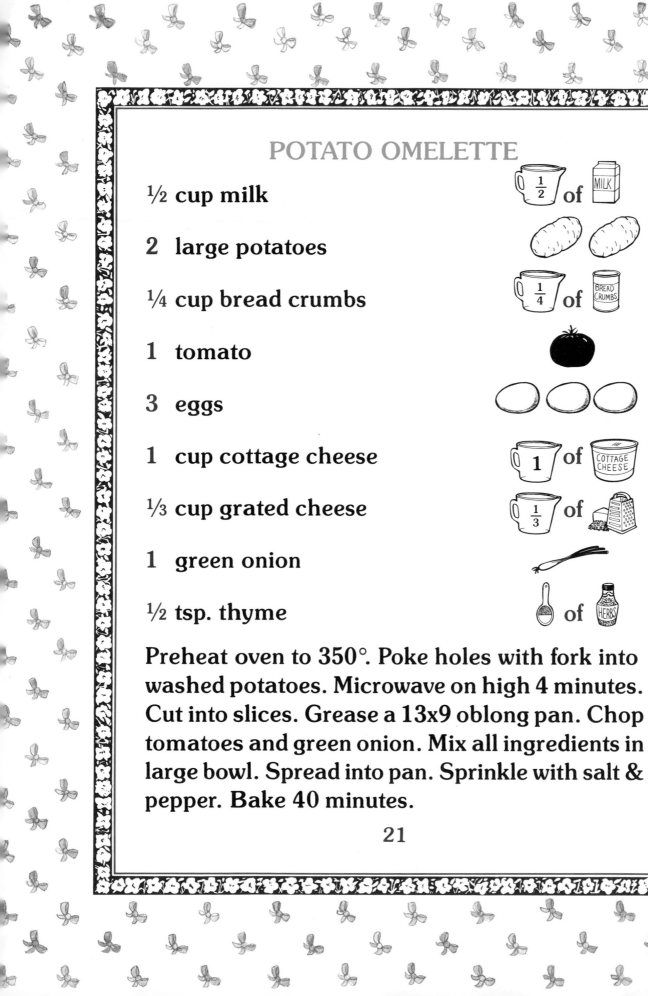

½ cup milk

2 large potatoes

¼ cup bread crumbs

1 tomato

3 eggs

1 cup cottage cheese

⅓ cup grated cheese

1 green onion

½ tsp. thyme

Preheat oven to 350°. Poke holes with fork into washed potatoes. Microwave on high 4 minutes. Cut into slices. Grease a 13x9 oblong pan. Chop tomatoes and green onion. Mix all ingredients in large bowl. Spread into pan. Sprinkle with salt & pepper. Bake 40 minutes.

FRENCH TOAST

1 egg

½ cup milk

2 slices bread

¼ teaspoon salt

1 tablespoon butter

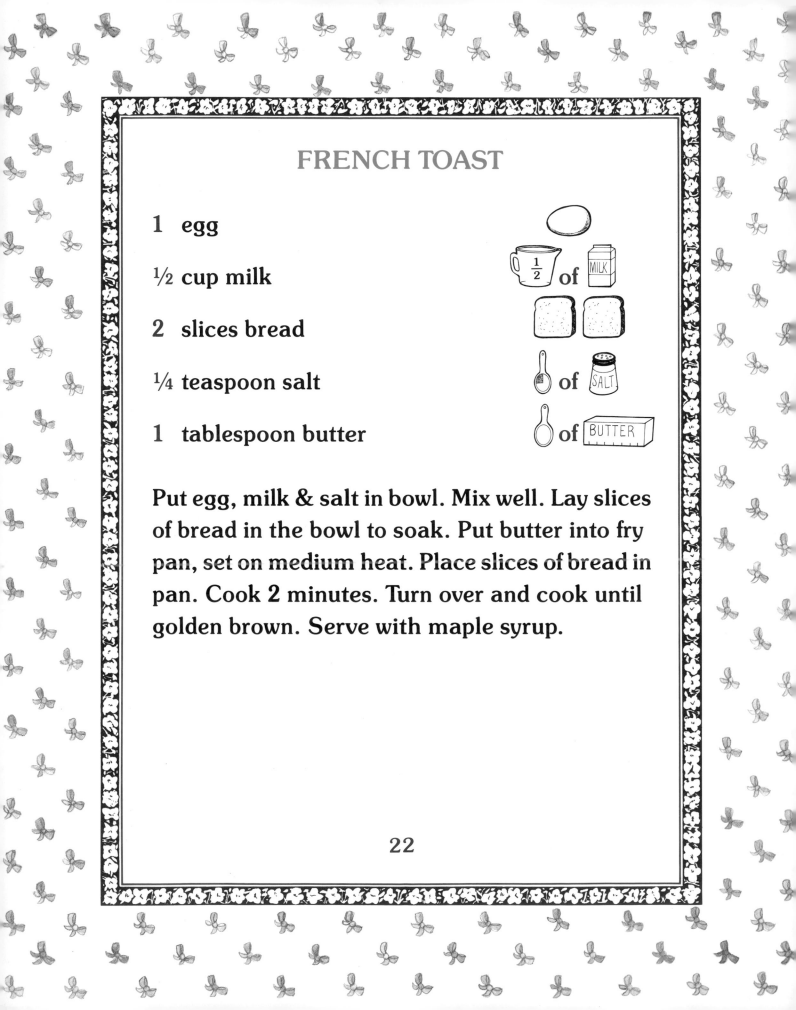

Put egg, milk & salt in bowl. Mix well. Lay slices of bread in the bowl to soak. Put butter into fry pan, set on medium heat. Place slices of bread in pan. Cook 2 minutes. Turn over and cook until golden brown. Serve with maple syrup.

APPLE PANCAKES

¾ cup milk

1 egg

2 tablespoons oil

1 cup flour

2 teaspoons baking powder

½ teaspoon salt

2 tablespoons sugar

1 apple, chopped fine

Beat in large bowl: milk, egg and oil. Add remaining ingredients. Stir lightly. Grease a large fry pan and set on medium heat. Pour ¼ cup batter to form each pancake. Cook until bubbles form on top. Turn over. Cook until golden brown. Serve with maple syrup.

23

BLACKBERRY COFFEECAKE

2 cups flour

2 teaspoons baking powder

⅔ cup milk

⅓ cup sugar

1 egg

¼ cup oil

2 teaspoons cinnamon

1 cup blackberries

⅓ cup brown sugar

Preheat oven to 375°. Put in large bowl: flour, baking powder, milk, sugar, egg, oil and cinnamon. Stir 25 strokes. Lightly stir in berries. Grease round cake pan. Pour in batter. Sprinkle brown sugar on top. Bake 35 minutes.

BLUEBERRY MUFFINS

½ cup sugar   ½ of SUGAR

2 cups flour   2 of FLOUR

1 teaspoon cinnamon   of CINNAMON

1 tablespoon baking powder   of BAKING POWDER

2 eggs

1 cup milk   1 of MILK

1 cup blueberries   1 of

5 tablespoons butter   of BUTTER

3 tablespoons brown sugar   of BROWN SUGAR

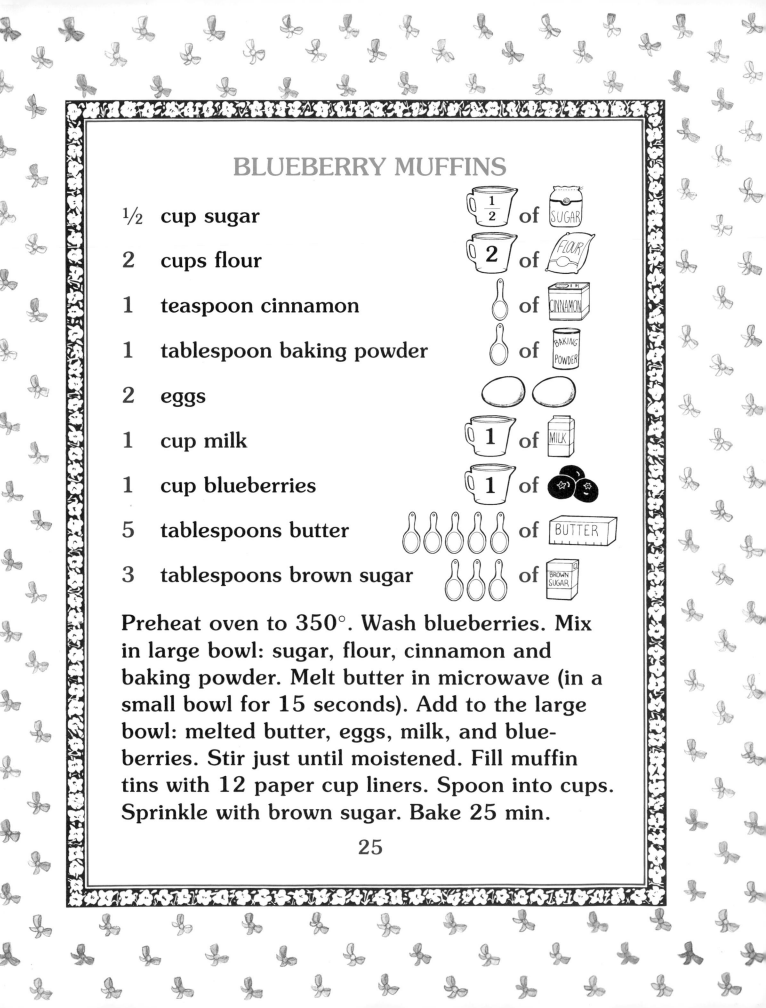

Preheat oven to 350°. Wash blueberries. Mix in large bowl: sugar, flour, cinnamon and baking powder. Melt butter in microwave (in a small bowl for 15 seconds). Add to the large bowl: melted butter, eggs, milk, and blueberries. Stir just until moistened. Fill muffin tins with 12 paper cup liners. Spoon into cups. Sprinkle with brown sugar. Bake 25 min.

BANANA NUT BREAD

3 bananas

2 eggs

⅓ cup vegetable oil

¾ cup sugar

1 teaspoon baking soda

2 cups flour

½ cup chopped walnuts

1 teaspoon cinnamon

½ cup water

Preheat oven to 350°. Butter a loaf pan. Put peeled bananas in a large mixing bowl. Mash well with a fork. Add in eggs, water and oil. Stir well. Add sugar, baking soda, flour, nuts and cinnamon, stirring just until blended. Don't over beat! Pour batter into the pan and bake 45 min.

26

BREAD STICKS

1 package of Refrigerator Biscuit soft bread sticks

2 tablespoons olive oil

¼ cup parmesan cheese (grated)

3 tablespoons sesame seeds

salt

Preheat oven to 350°. Open package and separate the 8 bread sticks. Twist each strip and place on an ungreased cookie sheet, pressing each end down firmly. Brush with olive oil, sprinkle with parmesan cheese, sesame seeds and salt. Bake 18-20 minutes until golden brown.

EASY CORN BREAD

1 cup cornmeal

1 cup flour

½ teaspoon salt

⅓ cup sugar

1 tablespoon baking powder

½ cup milk

½ cup sour cream

⅓ cup oil

1 egg

Preheat oven to 375°. Butter an 8″ square or round pan. In a large mixing bowl combine cornmeal, flour, salt, sugar and baking powder. Stir with spoon. Stir in milk, sour cream, oil and egg. Stir just until moistened. Don't over beat. Pour into pan. Bake 30 minutes.

WENDY'S GARLIC BREAD

1   loaf sourdough or french bread

5   tablespoons butter, softened

1   garlic clove

paprika

½   cup parmesan cheese

Preheat oven to 350°. Peel and chop garlic. In a medium bowl mix together garlic and softened butter. Add in paprika and half of the parmesan cheese. Cut bread in half lengthwise. Spread with garlic butter. Sprinkle with remaining parmesan and paprika. Place on cookie sheet. Bake 8 minutes.

NANCY'S BASIL BISCUITS

⅓ cup chopped fresh basil

1 stick butter

2 cups flour

½ cup grated parmesan cheese

2 teaspoons baking powder

½ teaspoon baking soda

¾ cup unflavored yogurt

Preheat oven 400°. Cut butter into slices and put into large bowl with flour, parmesan, baking powder and soda. Rub mixture with your fingers until coarse crumbs form. Stir in chopped basil and yogurt. Pat dough into a ball and place onto a lightly floured cutting board. Knead 10 times. Pat dough to form a log. Cut into 7 round biscuits. Place in a greased cake pan. Brush tops with olive oil. Sprinkle with extra parmesan. Bake 32 minutes.

CHAPTER 2

Soup & Sandwiches

CREAMY CLAM CHOWDER

2 small cans of chopped clams

1 big potato

1 small can evaporated milk

1 can chicken broth

3 tablespoons flour

½ teaspoon thyme

a little salt & pepper

Peel and chop potato into little cubes. In a medium pot, mix together flour and evaporated milk. Open cans of clams and squeeze just the juice into pot, holding back the clams. Add all ingredients (except clams). Stir and cook 3 minutes on high. Turn heat to medium and cook 13 minutes. Stir in clams and serve.

CREAM OF MUSHROOM SOUP

10   mushrooms

½   small onion

2   tablespoons butter

½   teaspoon thyme

3   tablespoons flour

1   can chicken broth

1½   cups water

1   chicken bouillon cube

1   small can evaporated milk

½   teaspoon salt

Wash and chop mushrooms and onion. Place in a medium pot with butter and thyme. Cook and stir on medium heat until onion is soft. Sprinkle with flour. Cook and stir a minute. Slowly add water, stirring constantly. Add all remaining ingredients. Cook 10 minutes.   33

CHICKEN NOODLE SOUP

1   can chicken broth

2   cups water

½   cup wide egg noodles

1   chicken breast or leftover chicken

1   cup frozen green peas

2   chicken bouillon cubes

2   tablespoons chopped parsley

1   carrot

Cut up chicken breast. Wash and chop parsley. Peel and cut carrot into thin round slices. Pour chicken broth and water into medium pot and bring to a boil on high heat. Add all ingredients to the pot. Reduce heat to medium, cover pot and cook 15 minutes.

MOM'S TUNA BOATS

1   can tuna fish

2   tablespoons mayonnaise

½ cup chopped celery

paprika

4   hot dog rolls

Preheat oven to 350°. Toast hot dog rolls in oven for 4 minutes. Wash and chop celery. Open can of tuna and squeeze out liquid into the sink. Put tuna in a bowl. Mix in mayonnaise and celery. Stuff hot dog rolls with tuna mixture. Sprinkle with paprika.

PINWHEEL SANDWICHES

4 flour tortillas

½ avocado

1 small tomato

4 lettuce leaves

cream cheese

sliced chicken or turkey breast

slices of cheese

mustard

Wash the lettuce and tomato. Spread cream cheese on each of the tortillas. Cut avocado in half, remove pit, and peel. Slice the avocado and chop the tomato. On each tortilla, place: sliced meat, then spread with mustard, add a slice of cheese, avocado, tomato, and top with lettuce. Roll each tortilla tightly and wrap with plastic wrap. Refrigerate 1 hour. Remove wrap and slice each roll into 6 pieces. Place pinwheels onto serving plate.

TOMATO & CHEESE TOAST

4   slices of bread

olive oil

1   tomato

¼ cup cheddar cheese, grated

2   tablespoons grated parmesan cheese

garlic powder

salt and pepper

Preheat oven to 350°. Place bread on cookie sheet. Brush bread with a little olive oil. Chop tomato into small pieces. Mix the grated cheeses together. Sprinkle bread with tomatoes, cheese, a little garlic powder, salt and pepper. Bake 7 minutes. Cut in half.

CHAPTER 3

Salads & Party Drinks

POTATO SALAD

4 potatoes

2 tablespoons water

parsley (chopped fine)

¼ cup mayonnaise

½ teaspoon mustard

salt & pepper

paprika

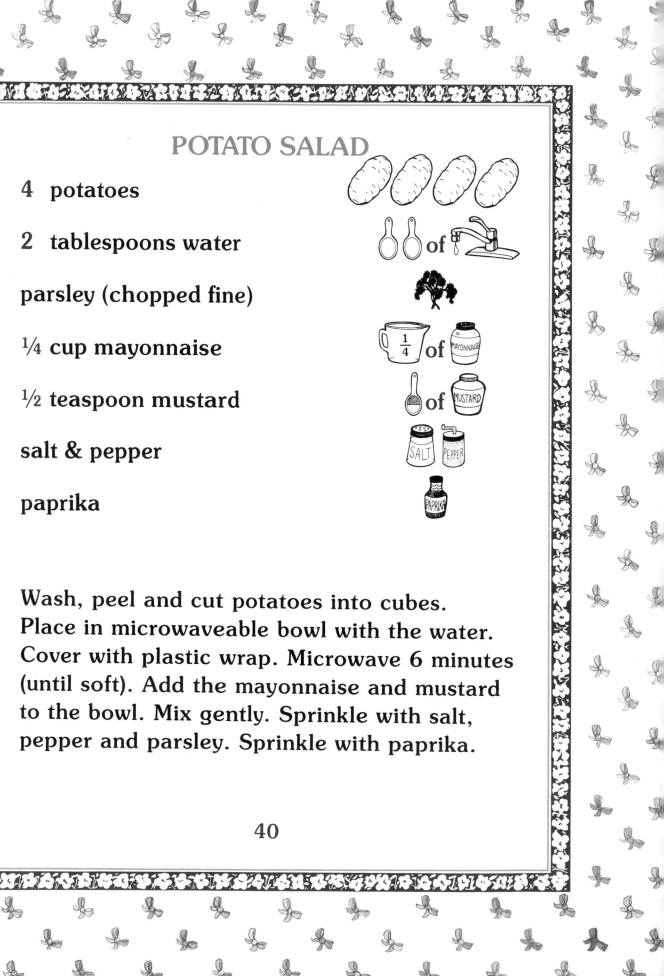

Wash, peel and cut potatoes into cubes.
Place in microwaveable bowl with the water.
Cover with plastic wrap. Microwave 6 minutes
(until soft). Add the mayonnaise and mustard
to the bowl. Mix gently. Sprinkle with salt,
pepper and parsley. Sprinkle with paprika.

FRUIT SALAD

1 banana

1 apple

1 orange

2 tablespoons brown sugar

1 dash cinnamon

2 teaspoons lemon juice

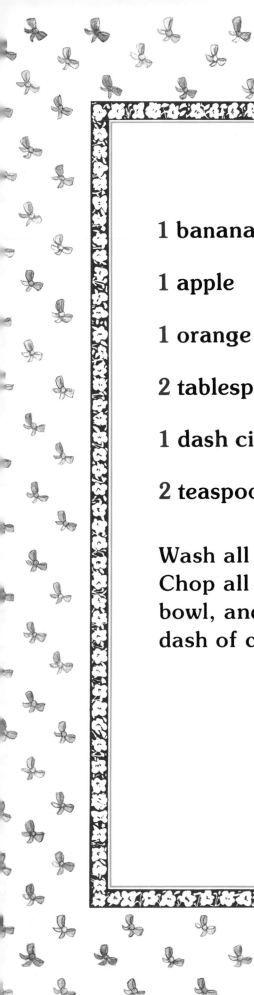

Wash all fruits. Peel the banana and orange. Chop all fruits into bite size chunks. Place in bowl, and add the sugar, lemon juice and a dash of cinnamon. Mix well and serve.

GREEN SALAD
WITH THOUSAND ISLAND DRESSING

1   egg

¼ cup mayonnaise

2   tablespoons ketchup

lettuce

2   tomatoes

3   mushrooms

salt & pepper

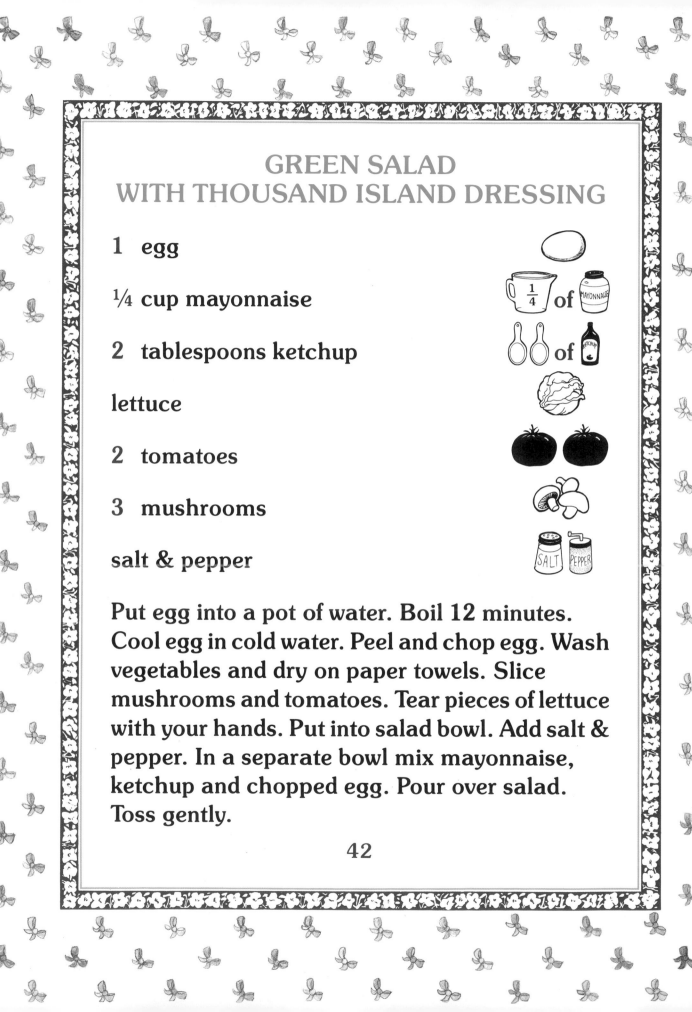

Put egg into a pot of water. Boil 12 minutes.
Cool egg in cold water. Peel and chop egg. Wash
vegetables and dry on paper towels. Slice
mushrooms and tomatoes. Tear pieces of lettuce
with your hands. Put into salad bowl. Add salt &
pepper. In a separate bowl mix mayonnaise,
ketchup and chopped egg. Pour over salad.
Toss gently.

BANANA SMOOTHIE

1   cup milk

1   banana

2   scoops vanilla ice cream

½ teaspoon vanilla

Put all ingredients into a blender. Blend until smooth.

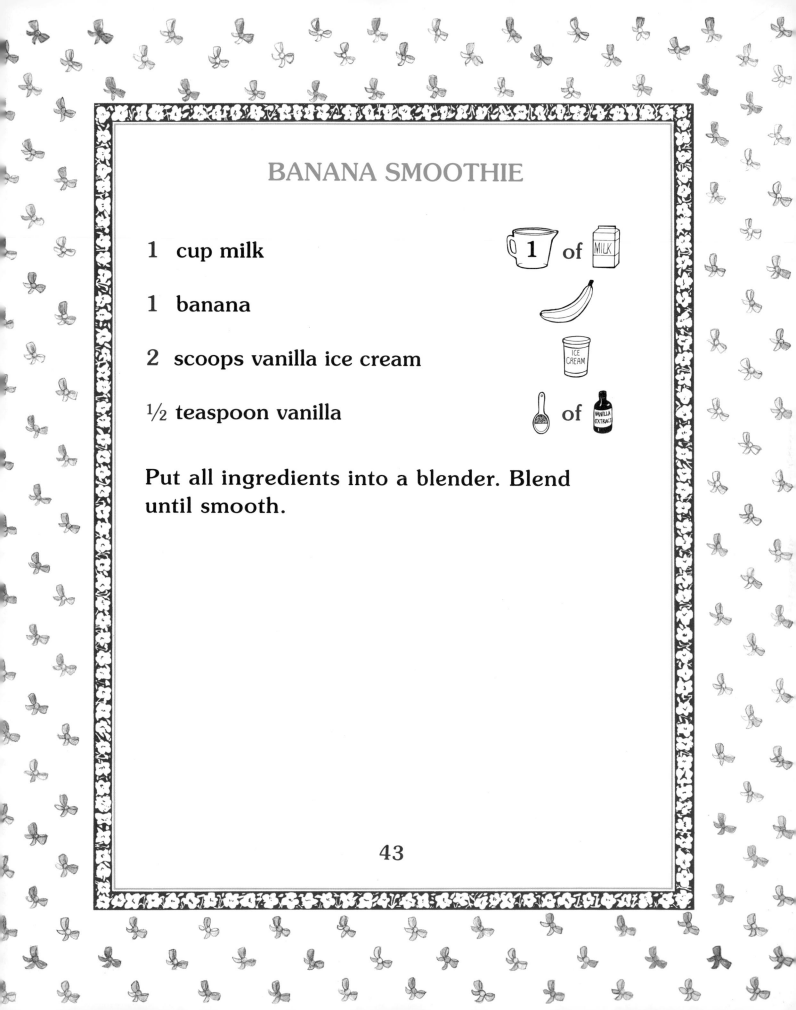

FRUITY FROST

1 cup fresh strawberries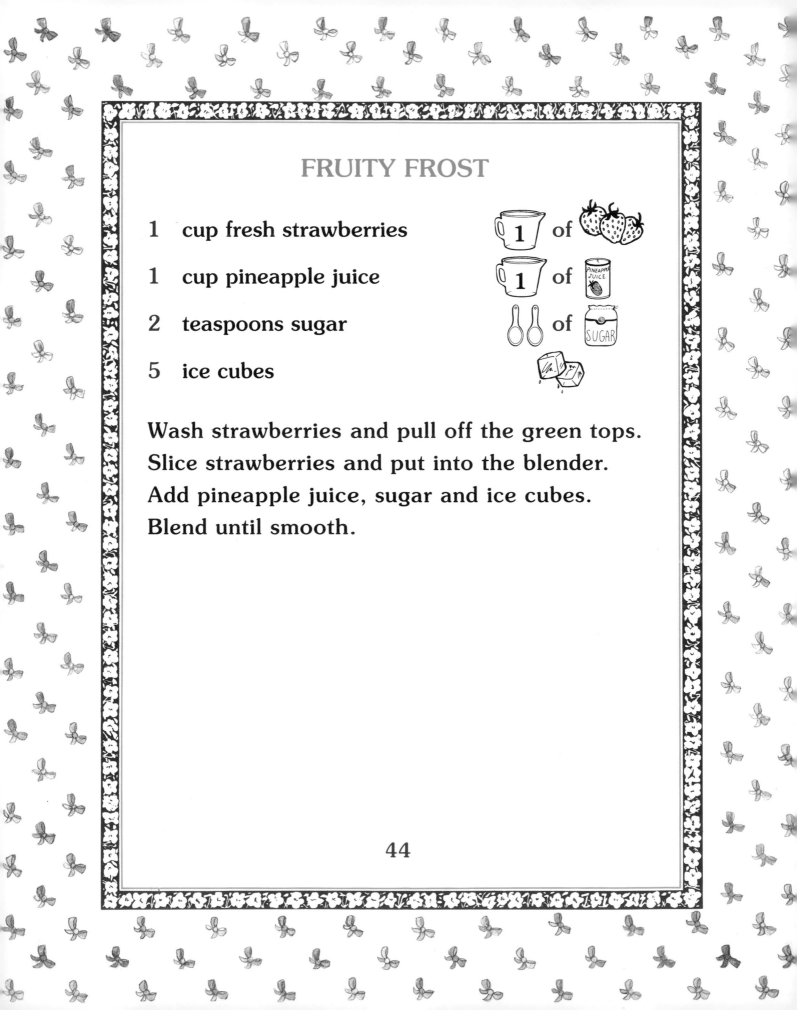

1 cup pineapple juice

2 teaspoons sugar

5 ice cubes

Wash strawberries and pull off the green tops.
Slice strawberries and put into the blender.
Add pineapple juice, sugar and ice cubes.
Blend until smooth.

CHAPTER 4

Main Dishes

SHAKE & BAKE SESAME CHICKEN

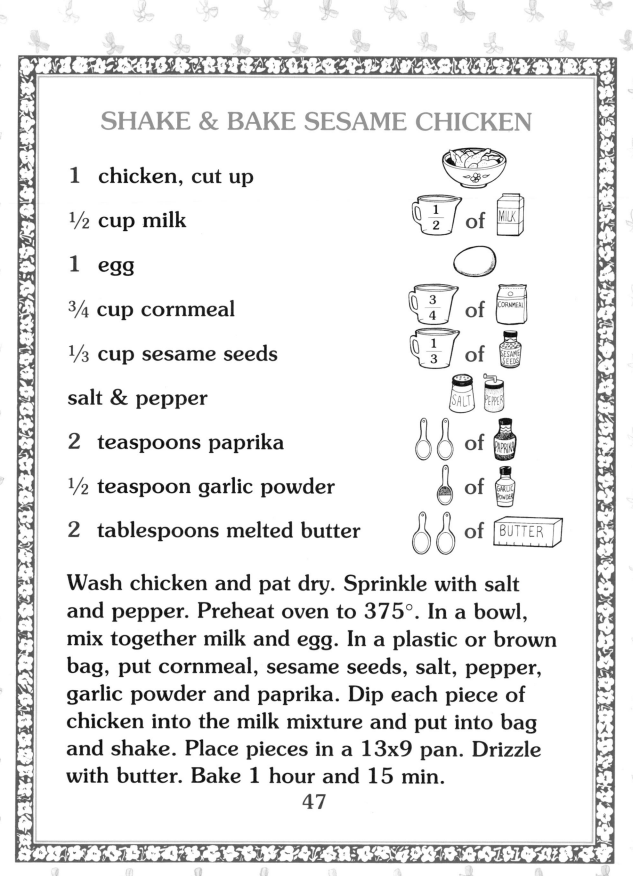

1 chicken, cut up

½ cup milk

1 egg

¾ cup cornmeal

⅓ cup sesame seeds

salt & pepper

2 teaspoons paprika

½ teaspoon garlic powder

2 tablespoons melted butter

Wash chicken and pat dry. Sprinkle with salt and pepper. Preheat oven to 375°. In a bowl, mix together milk and egg. In a plastic or brown bag, put cornmeal, sesame seeds, salt, pepper, garlic powder and paprika. Dip each piece of chicken into the milk mixture and put into bag and shake. Place pieces in a 13x9 pan. Drizzle with butter. Bake 1 hour and 15 min.

47

YUMMY ROAST CHICKEN & POTATOES

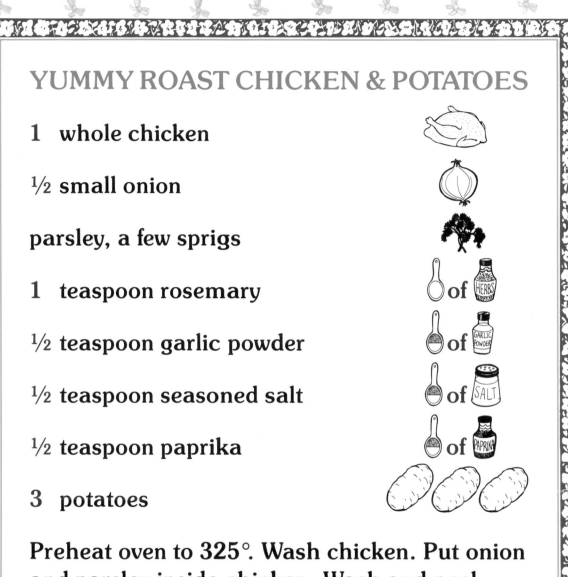

1 whole chicken

½ small onion

parsley, a few sprigs

1 teaspoon rosemary of HERBS

½ teaspoon garlic powder of GARLIC POWDER

½ teaspoon seasoned salt of SALT

½ teaspoon paprika of PAPRIKA

3 potatoes

Preheat oven to 325°. Wash chicken. Put onion and parsley inside chicken. Wash and peel potatoes. Cut each into 4 pieces. Put chicken and potatoes in a 13x9 pan. Brush chicken and potatoes with some olive oil, salt, pepper and paprika. Sprinkle chicken with rosemary, garlic powder and seasoned salt. Bake 1½ hours.

BARBECUED CHICKEN WINGS

12 chicken wings

salt & pepper

½ teaspoon garlic powder

1 teaspoon thyme

⅔ cup bottled barbecue sauce

Set oven at 325°. Place chicken wings in 13x9 oblong pan. Sprinkle with salt and pepper, garlic powder and thyme. Pour on barbecue sauce. Bake for 1 hour and 10 minutes.

BEEF STEW

1 lb. beef stew meat

3 carrots

3 potatoes

1 onion

2 cups water

2 bouillon cubes

⅓ cup flour

3 tablespoons ketchup

1 teaspoon herbs

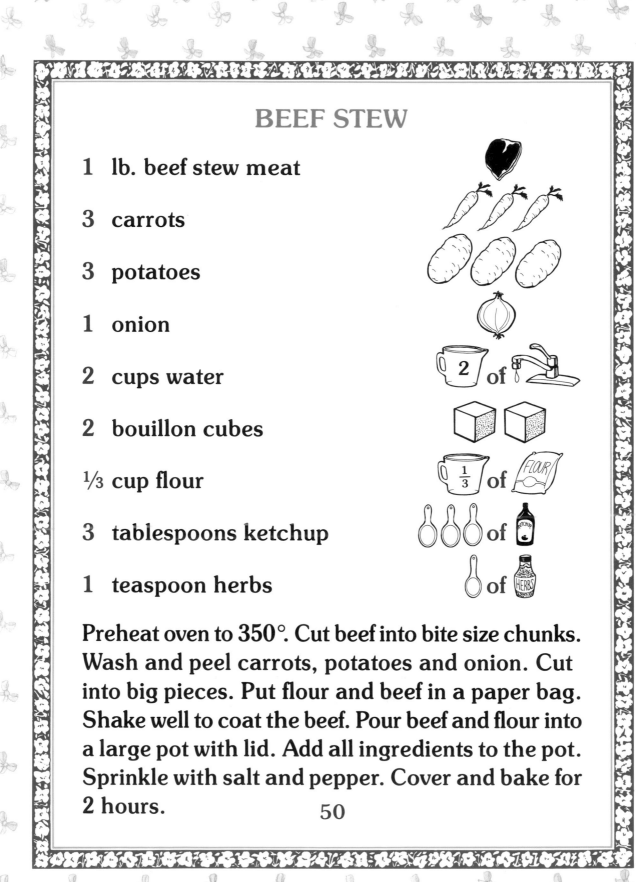

Preheat oven to 350°. Cut beef into bite size chunks. Wash and peel carrots, potatoes and onion. Cut into big pieces. Put flour and beef in a paper bag. Shake well to coat the beef. Pour beef and flour into a large pot with lid. Add all ingredients to the pot. Sprinkle with salt and pepper. Cover and bake for 2 hours.

BEST BURGERS

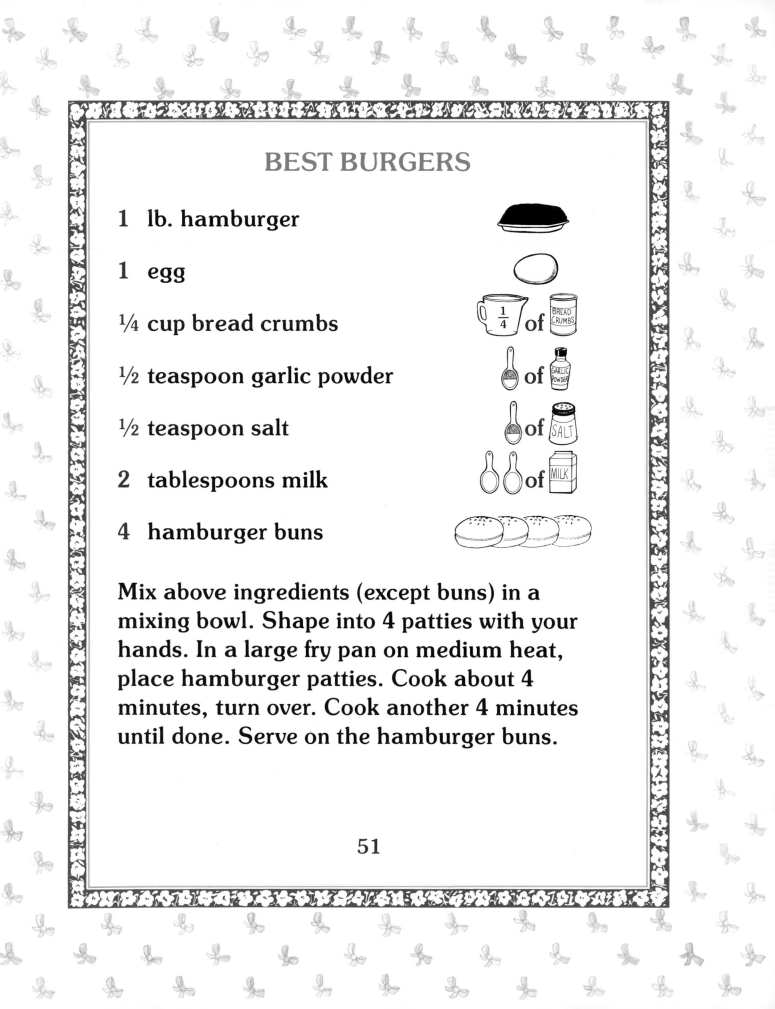

1   lb. hamburger

1   egg

¼ cup bread crumbs

½ teaspoon garlic powder

½ teaspoon salt

2   tablespoons milk

4   hamburger buns

Mix above ingredients (except buns) in a mixing bowl. Shape into 4 patties with your hands. In a large fry pan on medium heat, place hamburger patties. Cook about 4 minutes, turn over. Cook another 4 minutes until done. Serve on the hamburger buns.

MACARONI & CHEESE

2   cups macaroni

1½   cups milk

3   tablespoons flour

2   tablespoons butter

2   teaspoons mustard

1¼   cup grated cheddar cheese

3   slices bread

1   teaspoon salt

dash of pepper & paprika

Preheat oven to 375°. Cook macaroni in a pot of boiling water for 8 minutes. Drain. Grate cheese. In a microwaveable bowl, add milk, flour, butter, mustard, salt and ½ of the grated cheese. Stir. Microwave for 1 minute. Stir and microwave again for 1½ minutes. Stir. Put macaroni into the casserole dish. Pour sauce on top. Add remainder of cheese. Sprinkle with pepper & paprika. Bake 40 minutes.

TACOS

8 taco shells

½ lb. hamburger

2 small tomatoes

mild salsa

salt, pepper and seasoned salt

lettuce

black olives

cilantro

grated cheese (cheddar or jack)

Preheat oven to 350°. Chop tomatoes and cilantro. Tear lettuce into small pieces. Grate the cheese. Place taco shells on cookie sheet and bake 6 minutes. In fry pan, cook hamburger, breaking it up with a fork. Add a teaspoon of salsa; sprinkle on salt, pepper and seasoned salt. Stuff taco shells with a little meat, lettuce, tomatoes, cilantro, cheese & olives.

53

QUESADILLAS

6   flour tortillas

1½ cups grated cheddar or
    jack cheese (or mixture)

2   green onions

2   tomatoes

¼   cup sour cream

black olives

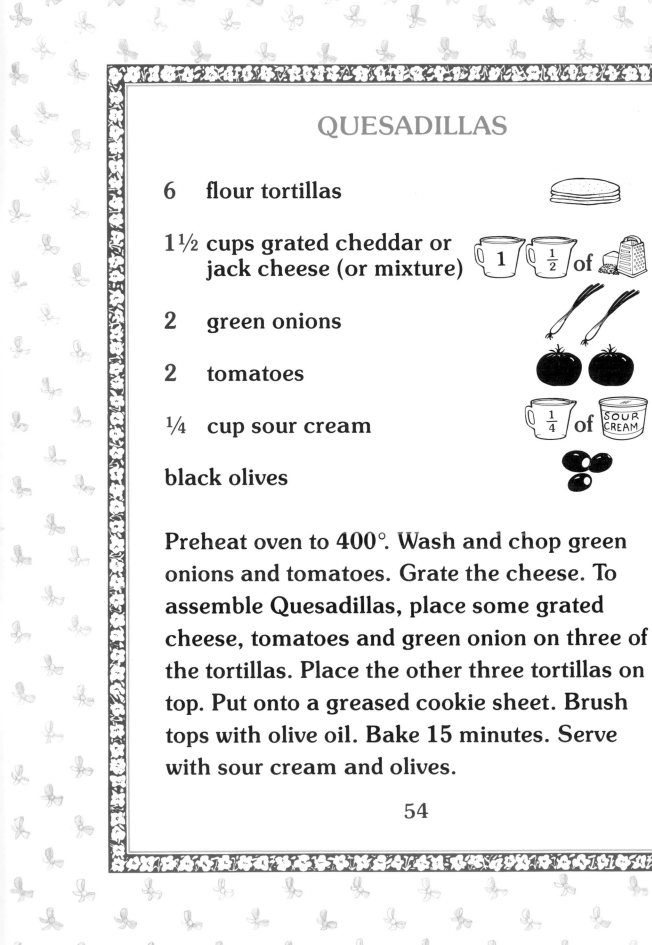

Preheat oven to 400°. Wash and chop green onions and tomatoes. Grate the cheese. To assemble Quesadillas, place some grated cheese, tomatoes and green onion on three of the tortillas. Place the other three tortillas on top. Put onto a greased cookie sheet. Brush tops with olive oil. Bake 15 minutes. Serve with sour cream and olives.

PARTY PIZZA

1   refrigerated all-ready pizza crust

½ lb. hamburger

½ teaspoon dried basil or oregano

1   clove garlic

1   cup grated mozzarella cheese

¼ cup grated parmesan cheese

¼ cup grated cheddar cheese

1   small can tomato sauce

Preheat oven to 425°. Grease a pizza pan or a 13x9 pan. Chop garlic. Cook hamburger and garlic in fry pan over medium heat. Add tomato sauce and herbs, salt and pepper. Cook on low for 5 minutes. Add 2 tablespoons water if sauce gets thick. Press out crust with hands into pan. Pour on sauce. Sprinkle with cheese. Bake 17 minutes.

TOPSY TURNOVERS

1 package frozen puff pastry shells

¼ lb. hamburger

¼ cup chopped parsley

2 tablespoons chopped onion

2 eggs

2 tablespoons bread crumbs

½ teaspoon salt

3 tablespoons parmesan cheese

Preheat over to 400°. Thaw puff pastry 20 minutes. Mix in bowl: hamburger, chopped parsley, chopped onion, 1 egg, bread crumbs, cheese, and salt. Stretch out each puff pastry shell with your hands to make a little larger. Put a spoonful of filling in the center of each. Fold pastry in half. Pinch edges with your fingers or fork to seal in filling. Place on a cookie sheet. Break remaining egg into cup & beat with a fork. Brush tops with the egg. Bake 25 minutes.

56

TUNA-NOODLE CASSEROLE

2   cups pasta (thin egg noodles)

1   can tuna, drained

1   can cream of mushroom soup

¼ cup milk

2   slices bread

¾ cup grated cheddar cheese

paprika

Preheat oven to 350°. Butter a casserole dish. Cook pasta in a pot of boiling water for 8 minutes. Drain in a strainer. Put pasta into casserole dish. Add tuna, soup, and milk. Cut bread into cubes and put on top of casserole. Spread cheese on top. Sprinkle with paprika and bake 25 minutes.

CHAPTER 5

Potatoes, Rice & Side Dishes

NICE RICE

1   cup rice

2   cups water

3   tablespoons ketchup

½ teaspoon garlic powder

2   chicken bouillon cubes

Put all ingredients into a pot with lid. Cook on high heat (covered) until rice almost comes to a boil. Turn burner down immediately to low and cook for 20 minutes. Don't lift lid until done. Remove from heat and let sit covered a few minutes.

MASHED POTATOES

3 large potatoes

2 tablespoons water

2 tablespoons butter

¼ cup milk

½ teaspoon salt

pepper

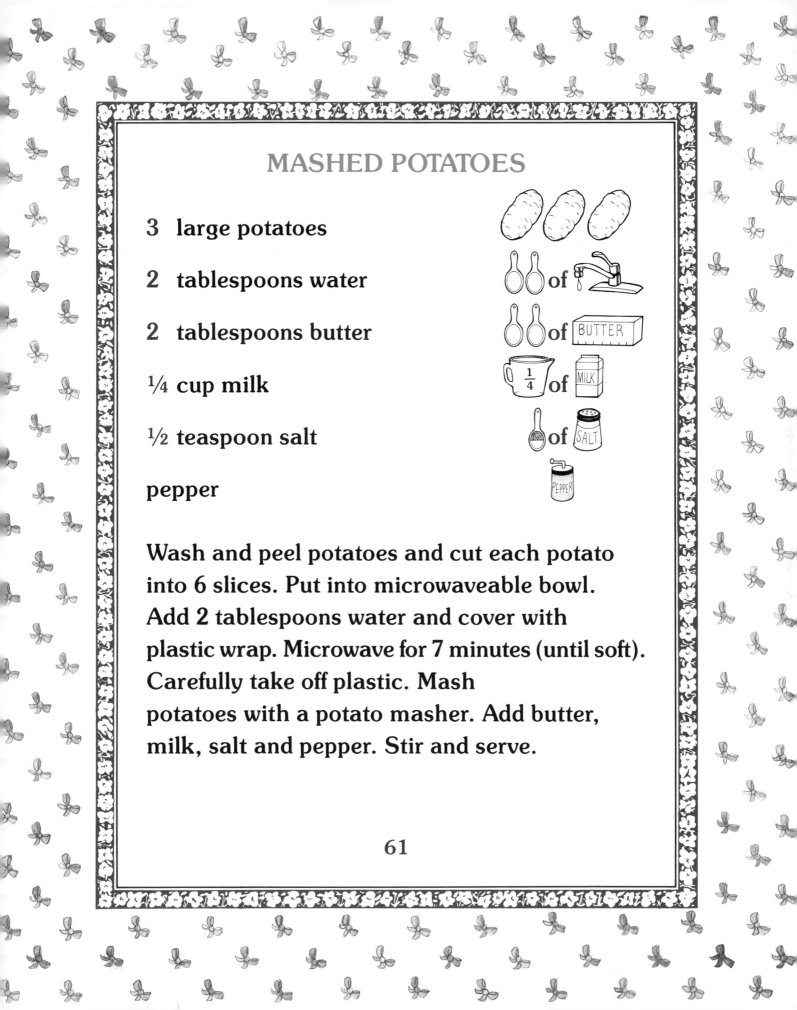

Wash and peel potatoes and cut each potato into 6 slices. Put into microwaveable bowl. Add 2 tablespoons water and cover with plastic wrap. Microwave for 7 minutes (until soft). Carefully take off plastic. Mash potatoes with a potato masher. Add butter, milk, salt and pepper. Stir and serve.

STUFFED MUSHROOMS

1   pound fresh mushrooms

1   small package frozen spinach

2   tablespoons melted butter

⅓ cup bread crumbs

½ cup crumbled feta cheese

⅓ cup grated parmesan cheese

1   egg

⅓ cup cottage cheese

1   tablespoon lemon juice

½ teaspoon salt

Preheat oven to 350°. Thaw spinach. Squeeze out water. Put spinach into mixing bowl. Wash mushrooms and pull off stems. Put mushroom caps on a cookie sheet and brush with melted butter. Combine all remaining ingredients into the bowl. Spoon some mixture in your hand and roll it into a ball. Place onto mushroom cap and press lightly. Sprinkle with extra parmesan. Bake 18 minutes.

EASY CARROTS

2   carrots

1   tablespoon water

1   tablespoon brown sugar

½   teaspoon salt

pepper

Wash and peel carrots. Slice into rounds (not too thick). Place carrots in microwaveable bowl. Add 1 tablespoon water, brown sugar, salt and pepper. Cover with plastic wrap and microwave about 3 minutes.

CHEESEY BROCCOLI

broccoli

½ cup cheddar cheese, grated

salt and pepper

Wash and chop broccoli. Grate cheese.
Place broccoli in a microwaveable bowl. Add 1
tablespoon water and cover with plastic wrap.
Microwave 4 minutes or just until cooked.
Sprinkle with salt and pepper. Add grated
cheese, and cover up again with the plastic
wrap. Let sit until cheese melts.

CHAPTER 6

Cookies, Cakes & Sweets

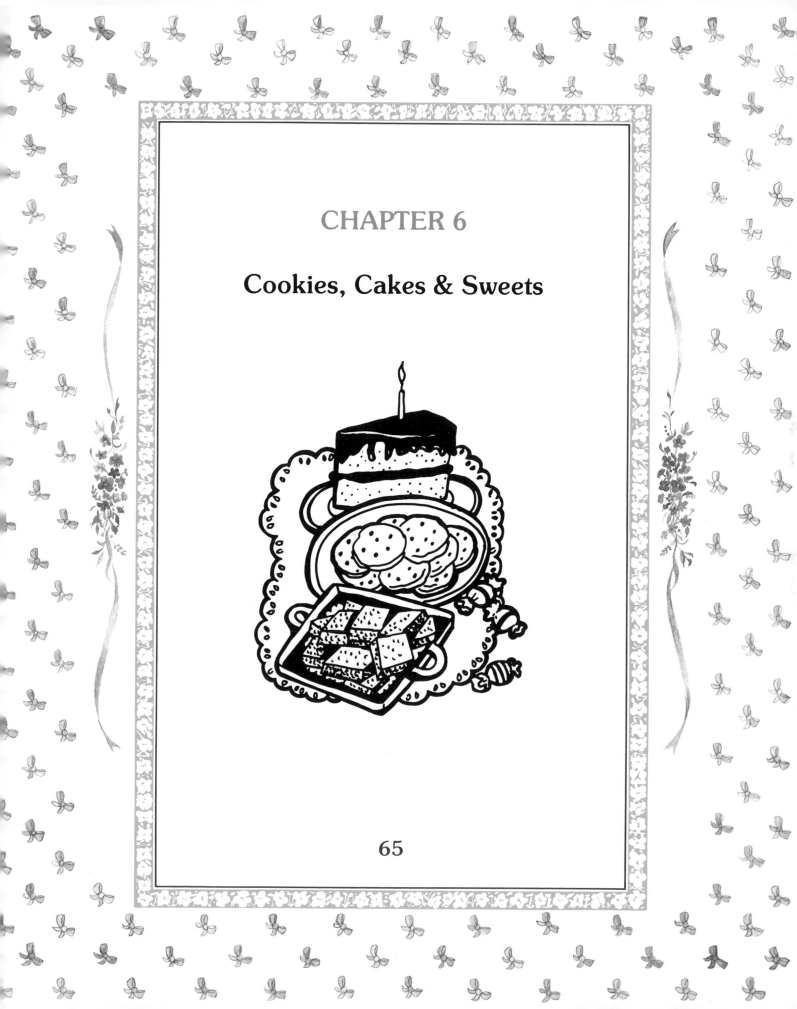

WENDY'S CHOCOLATE CHIP COOKIES

1½ sticks butter, softened

¾   cup peanut butter

¾   cup sugar

¾   cup brown sugar

2   eggs

2   teaspoons vanilla

1   teaspoon baking soda

2½ cups flour

1   big (12 oz.) pkg. chocolate chips

1   cup nuts

Preheat oven to 350°. In large bowl, using mixer, beat butter and peanut butter. Slowly add both sugars. Beat in egg and vanilla, Stir in flour and baking soda. Blend in chocolate chips and nuts. Drop by large teaspoonsful onto greased cookie sheet. Bake 12 minutes.

LEMON GLAZE CAKE

1   package yellow cake mix

1   small package vanilla pudding

1   cup water

4   eggs

⅓   cup vegetable oil

1   cup powdered sugar

½   cup warm water

1   lemon

Preheat oven to 350°. Butter and flour a 13x9 pan. Shake out excess flour. Put cake mix into mixing bowl. Add pudding, 1 cup water, eggs and oil. Beat 2 minutes with mixer. Pour into pan. Bake for 35 minutes. For glaze: cut lemon and squeeze juice into small microwaveable bowl. Add sugar and ½ cup water. Microwave 2 minutes. Pour glaze over cake.

ANTS ON A LOG

2 stalks of celery

peanut butter

raisins

Wash celery. Cut each stalk into 3 pieces. Spread peanut butter on celery and level it off with the straight edge of a table knife. Place raisins on top and serve.

MARSHMALLOW CRISPIE TREATS

6 cups crisp rice cereal

4 tablespoons butter

1 package of mini marshmallows

½ cup peanut butter

1 large bag chocolate chips

½ cup coconut

½ cup chopped nuts

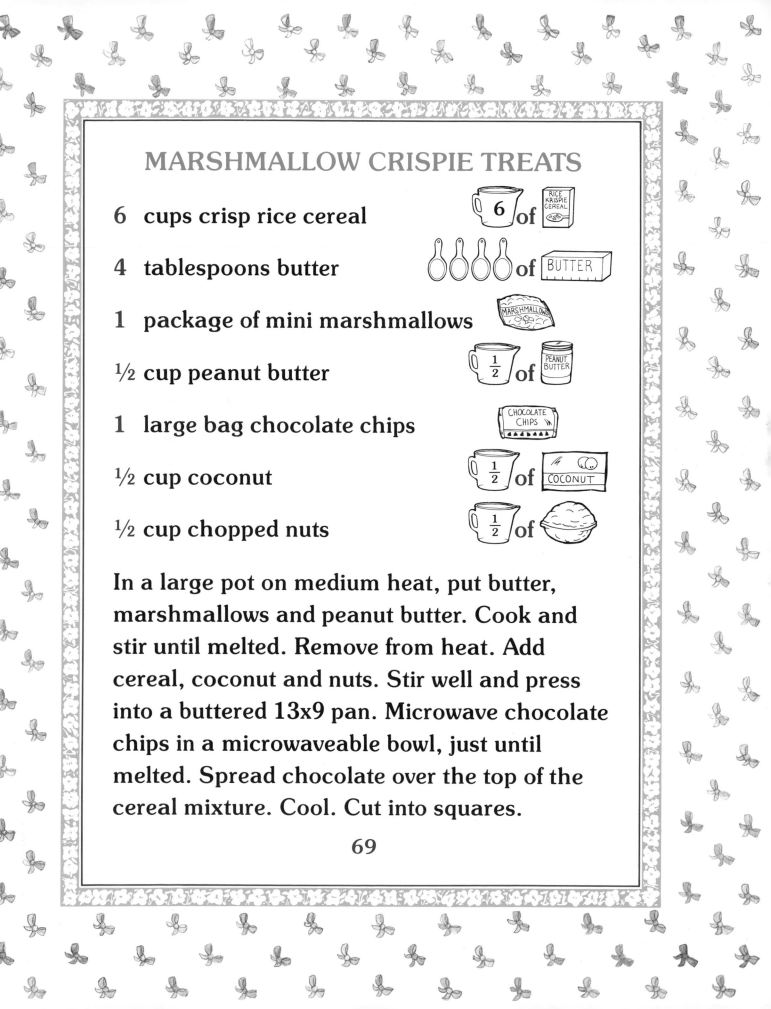

In a large pot on medium heat, put butter, marshmallows and peanut butter. Cook and stir until melted. Remove from heat. Add cereal, coconut and nuts. Stir well and press into a buttered 13x9 pan. Microwave chocolate chips in a microwaveable bowl, just until melted. Spread chocolate over the top of the cereal mixture. Cool. Cut into squares.

OLD FASHIONED GINGER SNAPS

½ cup shortening

1 cup sugar

1 egg

⅓ cup molasses

2 cups flour

2 teaspoons baking soda

2 teaspoons ginger

1 teaspoon cinnamon

Preheat oven to 350°. Put shortening and sugar in a large bowl. Beat well. Add eggs and molasses and beat until light. Stir in flour, baking soda, ginger and cinnamon. Roll pieces of dough into small balls. Place onto a greased cookie sheet. Sprinkle the tops with a little white sugar. Bake 12-14 minutes.

APPLE CRISP

4 apples

2 teaspoons lemon juice   of

1 teaspoon vanilla   of

5 tablespoons butter   of

½ cup brown sugar   of

½ cup flour   of

1 teaspoon cinnamon   of

½ cup nuts   of

ice cream

Preheat oven to 350°. Wash and cut apples into thin slices. Put slices into a greased pie pan. Sprinkle apples with lemon and vanilla. Toss gently with your hands. In a bowl, combine butter, brown sugar, flour & cinnamon. Mix with your fingers until it forms a paste. Stir in nuts. Sprinkle topping over apples. Bake 45 min. Serve with a scoop of ice cream.

71

TROPICAL BANANA TREAT

2 bananas

1 orange

¼ cup brown sugar

1 teaspoon butter

vanilla ice cream

Put butter in fry pan set on medium heat. Peel bananas and cut in half lengthwise. Place into pan. Add brown sugar. Cut orange in half and squeeze all the juice into pan. Gently shake pan and cook 4 minutes. Serve over ice cream.

ORANGE SHERBET CUPS

2 oranges

1½ cups orange sherbet

Let sherbet soften in a bowl. Cut tops off oranges. Hollow out all juice and pulp. Place shells in freezer. Add a spoonful of the orange juice to sherbet. Beat with mixer until fluffy. Spoon sherbet into orange shells; piled high. Put on orange tops and return to freezer until firm.

OLD FASHIONED FUDGE

6   **tablespoons butter**

⅓   **cup peanut butter**

4   **tablespoons milk**

1   **tablespoon vanilla**

3¼ **cups powdered sugar**

½   **cup brown sugar**

½   **cup cocoa**

½   **cup nuts, chopped**

Butter an 8" square pan. Put all ingredients, except nuts, into a medium pot. Cook over low heat for 7-8 minutes, while stirring constantly. Fudge should be smooth and fluffy. Stir in nuts and pour into square pan. Refrigerate. Cut into squares.

CHOCOLATE PEANUT BUTTER CHIP COOKIES

1½ sticks butter, softened

½ cup brown sugar

1½ cups sugar

2 eggs

2 teaspoons vanilla

2 cups flour

1 teaspoon baking soda

¾ cup cocoa

1 big package of peanut butter chips

½ cup chopped walnuts

Preheat oven to 350°. In a mixing bowl, beat together brown sugar and butter on low speed until creamy. Slowly beat in white sugar, eggs and vanilla. Beat well. Stir in with a spoon: flour, baking soda and cocoa. Mix well. Add chips and nuts. Drop cookie batter by spoonfuls onto an ungreased cookie sheet. Bake 9 minutes.

FANTASY FRUITS

2 cups strawberries

2 bananas

1 small package chocolate chips

2 tablespoons solid
vegetable shortening

Wash strawberries and dry very well on paper towels. Peel banana and cut into large chunks. Melt together chocolate and shortening in the microwave, just until melted. Dip each piece into the chocolate, covering one half of the fruit. Place onto cookie sheet lined with foil. Refrigerate.

STAINED GLASS SUGAR COOKIES

½   cup shortening   of

½   cup sugar   of

¼   cup brown sugar   of

1   egg

2   tablespoons maple syrup   of

2   teaspoons vanilla   of

1½   cup flour   of

1   teaspoon baking powder   of

12   colored hard candies, crushed

Put shortening, white and brown sugar into a large bowl. Beat until creamy. Add egg, syrup, and vanilla. Beat until fluffy. Stir in flour, baking powder. Shape dough into a big ball. Wrap in plastic wrap and refrigerate 1 hour. Preheat oven to 375°. Roll teaspoons of dough into small balls. Roll each in some white sugar. Place on ungreased cookie sheet. Press a criss-cross on top of each cookie using a fork. Decorate cookies with the hard candies. Bake 10 minutes.

DIVINE PEANUT BUTTER BALLS

1½ cups creamy peanut butter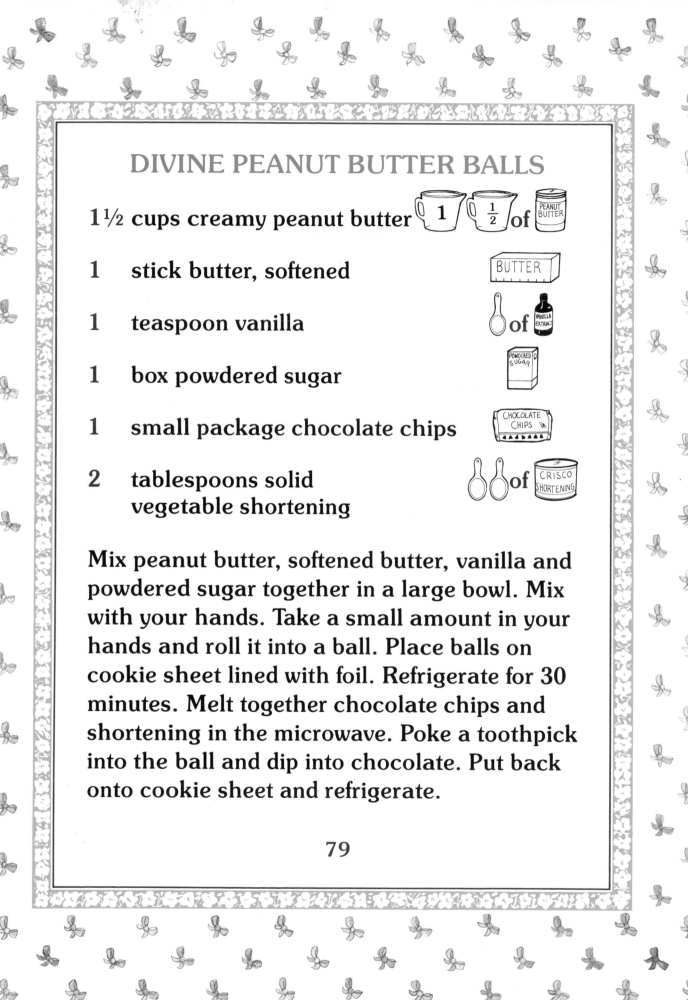

1   stick butter, softened

1   teaspoon vanilla

1   box powdered sugar

1   small package chocolate chips

2   tablespoons solid
      vegetable shortening

Mix peanut butter, softened butter, vanilla and powdered sugar together in a large bowl. Mix with your hands. Take a small amount in your hands and roll it into a ball. Place balls on cookie sheet lined with foil. Refrigerate for 30 minutes. Melt together chocolate chips and shortening in the microwave. Poke a toothpick into the ball and dip into chocolate. Put back onto cookie sheet and refrigerate.

CARAMEL POPCORN

⅓ cup popcorn

2 tablespoons oil

2 cups nuts

1 cup brown sugar

½ cup corn syrup

1 stick butter

1 teaspoon vanilla

½ teaspoon baking soda

Preheat oven to 275°. Pop the popcorn with the oil. Pour into a large roasting pan. Add nuts. Bring to a boil over low heat (an adult should help), stirring constantly, brown sugar, corn syrup and butter. Boil 5 minutes without stirring. Carefully remove from heat. Stir in vanilla and baking soda. Pour over popcorn. Stir. Bake 1 hour. Cool.

7 LAYER COOKIES

1½ cups graham cracker crumbs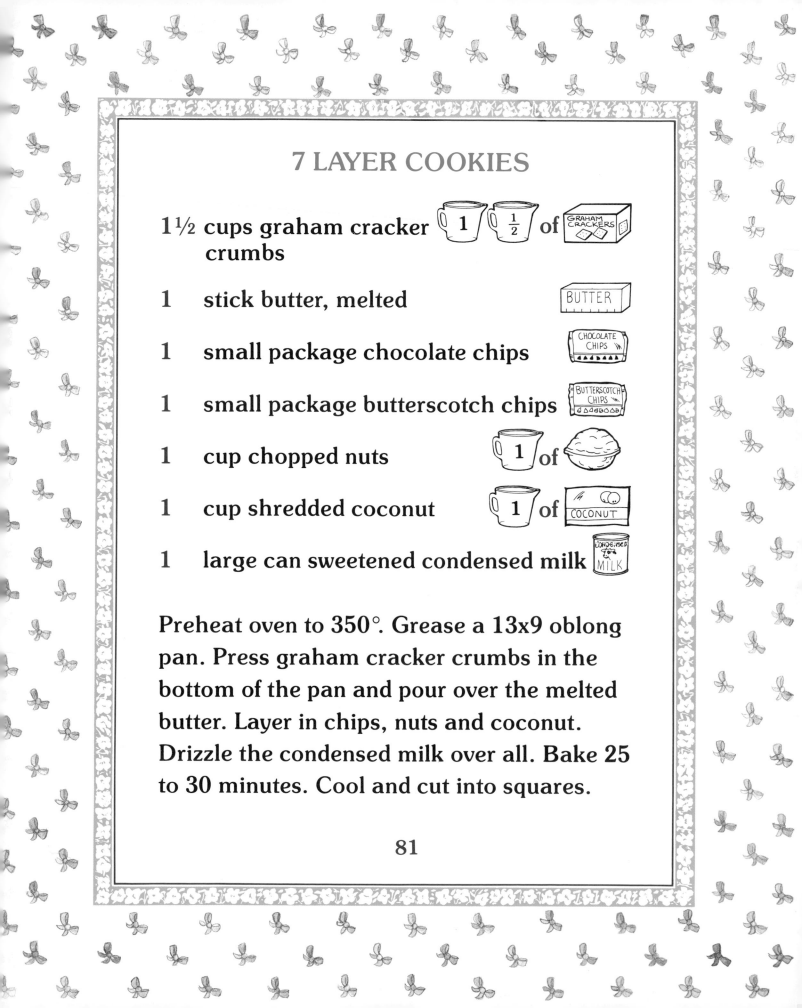

1 stick butter, melted

1 small package chocolate chips

1 small package butterscotch chips

1 cup chopped nuts

1 cup shredded coconut

1 large can sweetened condensed milk

Preheat oven to 350°. Grease a 13x9 oblong pan. Press graham cracker crumbs in the bottom of the pan and pour over the melted butter. Layer in chips, nuts and coconut. Drizzle the condensed milk over all. Bake 25 to 30 minutes. Cool and cut into squares.

RECIPE INDEX

Breakfast & Breads

Sunshine Eggs 20
Potato Omelette 21
French Toast 22
Apple Pancakes 23
Blackberry Coffeecake... 24
Blueberry Muffins 25
Banana Nut Bread 26
Bread Sticks 27
Easy Corn Bread... 28
Wendy's Garlic Bread 29
Nancy's Basil Biscuits 30
Golden Raisin Scones 16

Soup & Sandwiches

Creamy Clam Chowder... 32
Cream of Mushroom Soup 33
Chicken Noodle Soup 34
Mom's Tuna Boats 35
Pinwheel Sandwiches... 37
Tomato & Cheese Toast.. 38
Tea Party Sandwiches.. 15

Salads & Party Drinks

Potato Salad 40
Fruit Salad 41
Green Salad with Thousand Island Dressing 42
Banana Milk Shake 43
Fruity Frost 44

Main Dishes

Shake & Bake Sesame Chicken 47
Yummy Roast Chicken & Potatoes 48
Barbecued Chicken Wings 49

RECIPE INDEX

Beef Stew 50
Best Burgers 51
Macaroni & Cheese 52
Tacos 53
Quesadillas 54
Party Pizza 55
Topsy Turnovers 56
Tuna-Noodle Casserole 57

Potatoes, Rice & Side Dishes

Nice Rice 60
Mashed Potatoes 61
Stuffed Mushrooms 62
Easy Carrots 63
Cheesey Broccoli 64

Cookies, Cakes & Sweets

Wendy's Chocolate Chip Cookies 66
Lemon Glaze Cake 67
Ants on a Log 68
Marshmallow Crispie Treats 69
Old Fashioned Ginger Snaps 70
Apple Crisp 71
Tropical Banana Treat 72
Orange Sherbet Cups .... `73
Old Fashioned Fudge 74
Chocolate Peanut Butter Chip Cookies 75
Fantasy Fruits 77
Stained Glass Sugar Cookies 78
Divine Peanut Butter Balls 79
Caramel Popcorn 80
7 Layer Cookies 81
Cherry Cheesecake Pie 17

MY OWN RECIPES

_____
_____
_____
_____
_____
_____
_____
_____
_____
_____
_____
_____
_____
_____
_____
_____
_____
_____
_____
_____